Winning Audition Monologues for Teens and Adults

by

Nautic Von Horn

50

original monologues

for film, television & theatre auditions
1 – 2 minutes each

WINNING AUDITION MONOLOGUES

Copyright © 2022 Brent Nautic Von Horn

Contact the author at:

> Nautic Publishing
>
> Brent N. Von Horn
>
> https://www.nauticproductions.com
>
> email: nauticproductions@yahoo.com

Cover design by Nautic Productions © 2022 Brent N. Von Horn

Cover includes a photograph by Joanna Andrzejewska and a photograph by Roger Kirby (both provided by freeimages.com)

ISBN: 978-1-953479-02-0

First Edition, 2022

10 9 8 7 6 5 4 3 2 1

Other books by this author

Brent Nautic Von Horn is the author of the Doable Shakespeare Series, which adapts William Shakespeare's plays for modern actors and audiences without losing the beauty of the original language. Books in the series include:

- ***Doable Hamlet***
- ***Doable Romeo & Juliet***
- ***Doable Tempest***
- ***Doable Twelfth Night***
- ***Doable Midsummer Night's Dream***

Additionally, Mr. Von Horn has written *A Newbie's Cheat Sheet for Filmmakers* which is a comprehensive guide for all beginning filmmakers.

For more about the author's current acting, film, and writing projects, look him up on IMDb.com under the name Nautic Von Horn, or on his own site www.nauticproductions.com.

Introduction

Why do actors do monologues?

The best answer: because they're FUN. Slipping into a character's skin to be that character, live their life for a minute or so, make them come to life – it's a blast! It's addicting. The more you do, the more you want to do. Long or short, comedy or drama, contemporary or historical. It becomes a game in itself, to jump in and out of different characters.

Monologues do serve an important real-world function for actors. They help us get jobs. Whether as an in-person audition or a self-taped video, actors do monologues to show that they can act. That they can become a character and express that character's emotions, and transition between different emotions. That they can be *real* while pretending. Monologues are aimed primarily at casting directors because that's who we need to impress. The casting director sitting there in some stale audition room or before their computer, most likely terribly bored and depressed after already watching dozens of terrible auditions. They are ready to pull their hair out, wondering if the day will never end, if a good actor will never show up.

Casting directors are often maligned but consider for a moment what a difficult job they have. Producers and directors on one side, desperate for the CD to find the "perfect" actor for their project. With the average tv show costing One Million Dollars to produce, per episode, there is a lot of stress placed on finding the perfect actor for each role. And of course, directors and producers want that CD to find the right actors NOW! On the other side of the poor CD are thousands of wanna-be actors, begging for the parts even when they haven't prepared and trained as they should have. It's no wonder actors think most CD's are jerks!

But CD's are not jerks. They're just people with problems. I always tell my acting students, when you step into that audition room you must keep in mind that you are there to solve their problems. Presuming, of course, that you are the type of actor that has prepared and trained; if so, then you are what they've been waiting for!

When you perform, showing the CD how much fun you're having is a sure way to getting the job.

What is an Audition Monologue?

I disagree with Webster (and many acting instructors) on the definition of a "monologue." To some, it is any long speech. But to me it is vital that the speaking character be talking *to some other character*. The so-called monologue where an actor comes out and addresses the audience or just "speaks to the air" is, to me, more an example of performance art, or speech making, or even a public service announcement – but *not* a good piece for audition purposes because it doesn't prove to the CD that you can become a character. A monologue should fit into the larger story of a character's life, where the character lives and breathes. You inhabit them for a minute, but they must have lives before and after. They must seem real. In that character's world if they're talking, they must be talking *to someone*!

The following original monologues have been written for the sole purpose of providing actors with audition material that showcases an actor's abilities, to impress the CD, to get that actor a job. These monologues can all be altered however you may like, to change gender references, for example. I identify as male, so most of these are written for a "MAN" character, but there is no reason that most of them can't apply just as well to anyone else. You may also need to adjust the timing of a monologue, to run longer or shorter. Most of these are aimed at running between one and two minutes. Feel free to either add your own material to stretch out a monologue or cut lines as you need to make it shorter.

Provided with each monologue are notes on performing the piece. Hopefully helpful notes. Ultimately, however, when you perform a monologue, it must be *your* performance, *your* take on the material, and that means the notes on how I interpret them are at best a starting point for you.

I am providing these works for you to use. If you perform any of them publicly in anything other than an audition setting, all I ask is that you give me credit as the writer.

Let me say a bit about the order of these monologues: there is none. You might expect groupings of "comedy" or "dark" or "romantic", but all such labels fail when one considers that there is comedy in the darkest drama, and drama in the funniest comedy. We don't live in a black-and-white world, and neither should your characters.

Look through these monologues until you find one that "calls" to you; you'll know it when it happens. It's up to you, then, to choose how you will perform it, what emotions the character feels, what actions fit best. That's the fun of it.

Have fun. Acting isn't easy – anyone who tells you so is lying. But it is FUN!

~ Nautic Von Horn

This book is dedicated to all those who believed
in me and encouraged my acting,
and to those that didn't.

How to perform winning audition monologues

The Audition Process

When I've worked as a casting director, I have been *astounded* at how bad actors can be. Actors are bad, usually, due to a lack of preparation – not a lack of talent.

Too many actors fail to take classes, fail to push themselves to improve, fail to train, fail to practice. And it shows.

When you audition, if you know what you are doing it is clear right away to the CD. And vice versa, unfortunately. From literally the first words out of your mouth.

So, let's get this clear. When you enter an audition room or start your self-tape (same thing), it's up to you to make a good first impression immediately. I've seen actors walk in with a deer-in-the-headlights look on their face as they hesitatingly step toward the CD, saying. "Uh … hi. Is this … should I stand here? You want me in the middle here? Should I start? Are you ready?" Come on, people! That's enough to make any CD pull their hair out. The CD knows immediately that the next few minutes will be a total waste of their time. No wonder so many CD's sit there half ignoring actors, maybe picking at their nails or doing a crossword puzzle. The CD's attitude is simple: if you don't know what you're doing, then you are not ready to be in the audition room.

Starting a self-tape audition poorly is even worse, because while a CD may not kick you out of the audition room before you finish, you can bet they will hit "delete" on your tape! They've always got lots of other tapes to watch.

So, what should you do?

When you walk in, you need to OWN that room. Walk in with confidence. If you're nervous, think of it this way: the CD has a huge problem – they must find a good actor – and you are there to solve that problem! You are the hero at that moment. Walk in and begin with the thought that they desperately want you to succeed.

Slate with confidence. "Slating" is what we call an actor's introduction of themselves. Something like, "Hello everybody! What's up? I'm Nautic Von Horn and I'm represented by Model and Talent Management." This is what you do FIRST, immediately upon entering the room (or starting your tape). It's your first impression, and first impressions count. Don't think of slating as an obligation – think instead that slating is your *opportunity* to make that good first impression.

Make your slate memorable. For example, "Hey everybody! Wow, it's great to be here today! I am Nautic Von Horn and I'm represented by Model and Talent Management." The more memorable you are, the better. If the CD remembers you after seeing fifty actors, then that's called *winning*! By the way, be sure to add your personal stuff to the beginning of your slate only. You want to finish with your name and the name of your talent agency.

After slating, move straight into your work. If you've been asked to prepare a monologue, then begin immediately. Do not muddle the situation with any editorializing, such as "This monologue is from such and such play" or "I'll start now" or "my character has just been in an accident." Just start the work.

And please, don't get into the bad habit of doing any ritualistic mumbo jumbo between your slating and your work. I've seen it all. From simply looking down and then back up, to spinning in a circle while rubbing your hands together. If you do anything like this to "get ready" what you're really telling the CD is that you can't become a character without doing such silly or superstitious stuff. That's not a good message. When you move straight from your happy slating into some other emotion for your character work, you get at least ten brownie points from the CD.

When you finish your work, say "Thank you" with the same level of cheerfulness that you slated with, and then head for the door. That's right, leave. They may stop you if they have questions, and that's good if they do, but by being prepared to leave quickly you are showing them that you respect their time.

That's the process. (1) slating; (2) performing; and (3) leaving.

Doing anything other than this shows that you need to work harder on your training.

Two Goals

You always have TWO goals when you audition. Most people only focus on the obvious first goal, that you are there to prove your acting abilities. But the second goal is just as important.

CD's know that the success of any given project can be derailed if there are negative personalities involved. Lots of good projects never get off the ground or get shelved along the way because of squabbles among the cast. And CD's also know that when a production fails because of one or two bad apples, the finger gets pointed back at the CD for recommending those actors! CD's will not roll the dice on you if they have any reason to think that you will be that kind of disruptive person on set.

Which is why your second goal is simply to show them how wonderful you are as a human being. How much fun you would be to work with. That you are a "people person" who gets along with everyone. That you would be cheerful and optimistic no matter how long the filming day is.

You accomplish this goal by slating with maximum cheerfulness, letting the best of your personality shine bright. If they ask any questions of you, answer positively. If your audition includes any improv where you need to make choices, make only positive, life-affirming, happy choices. Never go to the dark side.

For example, I sometimes ask for an improv-based audition where an actor may do anything they want, provided they begin with the words, "What's that smell?" Such things as farts and bad body odor frequently come up. But imagine the effect on the CD listening to you speak about farts. While it may be funny, that CD will (consciously or unconsciously) now associate you with a bad smell. Surely that's not what you want! So instead, make the CD think of chocolate chip cookies coming out of the oven, or something else wonderful; make them associate you with only good thoughts!

Performing

You (the actor) have one job, and only one job: you must bring characters to life. That is the essence of acting. And it's all about expressing the emotions of the character. Which means, your job is totally dependent upon your understanding of the character.

Always start with the script. Writers write with agonizing dedication to their craft, in order to best create their characters and the world in which their characters live. You must read the entire script, at least twice. It becomes clear that there is no such thing as a "small character" when one thinks about the writer's process. Every single character (indeed, every scene, and even every word) is in the script for a purpose. There are no "filler" parts. You must look at the whole story and understand how your character fits in. Ask yourself why your character is in there in the first place, why your character is important to the other characters and to the audience.

Scripts are always written sparingly. There will be some information about your character, and you can glean more from clues such as how other characters treat yours. But ultimately, a script will only be your beginning point. You need to dive deeper into your character than the words.

The "Five W's" will help you. Ask yourself who, what, when, where, and why.

Who is your character, and who are the other characters?

What is happening? And what is really happening (the subtext, in other words)?

When (time of day, period, before or after something, etc.) does this take place?

Where is your character, and how does being in that place affect your character?

And the biggest questions of all: why? Why is your character talking now? Why saying this? Why speaking with this person or that? Why is your character doing anything? Why is your character in this scene?

When we bring characters to life, it's all about expressing that character's emotions. You must understand your character at a deep enough level that you FEEL what the character is feeling. Make up the answers to the Five W's – make your choices and let them inform your acting.

Many actors decide what a character's emotion is and then tell themselves to do that emotion. For example, they decide to put on their "angry" face here, and their "sad" face there. But this is the tail wagging the dog. You'll likely seem shallow, and struggle with changing from one emotion to the next. Instead, do your homework and decide what the character is feeling at each point, and why. Then when you act think of the reasons why your character feels this way, feel for your character, become your character. If your character's outraged, you're outraged. If your character's in love, you're in love. When you feel, your own emotions will naturally drive your expressions and body language without the need to glue on anything you once saw in the mirror.

Good audition monologues have at least two emotions, some many more. This is important because not only does the CD need to see you expressing the emotion of a character, but they also need to see you transition from one emotion to the next. The CD knows the script and character that they're auditioning you for – you often don't – and they know the difficulty of the character. They will be watching to see that you have the training necessary to express the emotions of the script.

As you consider your character's emotions, don't forget the emotions of the other person your character is talking to. Your character needs to react to the other, so if your character is saying anything that would be causing the other to act or show anything, think about how that would in turn cause your character to respond. Although it's called a monologue ("mono". meaning one), you must always think about the other character(s)!

Relax. Decide how your character moves and let your character move in the space you have available. Don't be a frozen talking-head stiff. We humans communicate more through expressions, gestures, and body language than through words; be human. Make your character human. Be aware of what space you have available to work in (the camera "frame") and use that space fully.

Speaking of movement, being relaxed does not mean not moving. On the contrary, being relaxed means you have the freedom for *good* movement. Good movement is anything and everything that helps express who your character is and what they're feeling at that moment. *Bad* movement is everything else. For example, shifting your weight back and forth may indicate your character is nervous, and that movement may be a good choice for you if indeed your character is nervous. However, if you are shifting back and forth because YOU are nervous yourself, and not the character, then that is something you need to learn to control and stop. "To thine own self be true," said Shakespeare. Know yourself. Watch your videos critically, with an eye toward cutting out all bad movement, as well as learning to bring more good movement into your work.

Acting teachers debate the question of making eye contact. For me, it depends upon whether you are auditioning in person or through a self-tape. If in person, looking right into the CD's eyes can be awkward and intimidating. For that reason, most instructors advise that you pick a spot on the wall, just above and to one side of the CD, and perform as if the character you're talking to is there. But if you are self-taping where there's no fear of intimidating the CD, then in that case I highly urge you to look right into the camera lens. The reasons for this are simple. Making eye contact with the viewer results in more of your energy coming through. It's more effective, more powerful. The viewer will be more likely engaged with what you're doing and find it harder to look away. Your character's emotions will more strongly affect the viewer if you have good eye contact through the lens.

Please feel free to slow down. Why do so many beginning actors rush through their work? Perhaps they're nervous and want the audition over ASAP – but even if you are nervous, you certainly don't want to communicate that fact. Slow yourself down. Make sure you make the most of each beat. Don't throw anything away.

Use the power of a pause, if it fits your material. Sometimes called a "pregnant pause," your work may be most effective at the point when you are saying nothing. In a pause, where we are not distracted by the dialogue, we can really see and understand your character's emotion.

Choose your monologue wisely. Make sure it is right for you. Meaning that it is something you want to perform over and over, because of course you will be doing so. Meaning also that it is a piece you can sink your teeth into as an actor, where you can empathize with the character and feel that character's emotions. Consider the entertainment value of your monologue; it should catch the CD's attention and hold it.

Writing Your Own Monologue

You may, for many reasons, want to write your own monologue. Perhaps you can't find one that seems perfect for you, or for a certain audition. You may want a piece that fits a particular situation, for example if you are trying to convince a director that you would be perfect for a character in a book that director has optioned. Or you may just be reworking a monologue, to make it work better for you.

A monologue is a story. Like all good stories, it needs a beginning, middle, and end. The beginning should give us the set-up, while the middle raises stakes and the end resolves the situation.

Make it fun for you to perform, and fun for your viewers to watch. Not fun as in comedic, necessarily. Make sure it's something you want to perform again and again, something that other people will want to watch.

Remember, your character must be speaking to another character (or characters, plural). And show us the moment when the characters are in conflict.

Your character must have a goal, and the other character should be part of the problem that makes it hard for your character to reach that goal. When your character is engaging with the other, then you (as the actor) will find it much easier to feel your character's emotions. I see too many monologues where the character is simply telling a story, perhaps to their best friend. But the friend is just there to listen – that friend is not a meaningful part of the monologue. In almost all cases the solution is easy: instead of choosing to show us that moment when your character is telling their friend about something that happened, show us the moment when the character was actually living the underlying story's events. Instead of telling your friend how much you hate your mother, tell your mother!

Write your monologues in a way that gets quickly to the gut punch. Don't hold back. And remember, it's all about emotions.

Winning Audition Monologues for Teens and Adults

By Nautic Von Horn

I SHOT HIM RIGHTEOUSLY

Sheriff

The first man I ever killed was my oldest brother. He stole a horse and saddle. I was 16, part of an eight-man posse that included my pa, but it was me what pulled the trigger. I was a ten-day wonder. People bought me drinks, saloon dinners for free, just to tell the tale. How he ran and hid. How, when I found him, he pulled a six-gun but couldn't shoot his own brother. How I could.

My brother got a grave, out yonder. I got a badge, free room and board, money for meals, and I been your sheriff now more'n thirty years. So, yes, Mr. Prosecutor. Yes, Your Honor. I am a killer. I'm your killer, I'm the town's killer. And that's what keeps you honest simple folk safe, secure in your beds at night, knowing that rapists, thieves, murderers, cattle rustlers, bad evil men are kept away from you good people.

You want this job, Your Honor? Do you, Mr. Prosecutor? Does any of you? I didn't think so! So where do you get off telling me this shooting ain't justified? How do any of you sit here in judgment of me? I've killed a lot of men, all bad cuz I says they bad, and this man were just another. I shot him righteously. Hang me if you must.

NOTES:

This man is used to doing things his way. He's been Sheriff for 30 years in a small Western town, years ago in the "Old Wild West" where he could do pretty much whatever he wanted. His word was law. No one dared ever second guess him. He was a rough kid and has always been a rough "take no prisoners" sheriff. He sees the world in rigid black and white. Criminals are bad guys who deserve what they get. His brother stole a horse, so therefore his brother deserved to die. Period. No questions, no doubts. He believes law enforcement requires a man-of-action like himself.

But now he is shocked and pissed, because the system has questioned his power and authority. The townspeople objected to his latest shooting, and he's being tried for murder. The Prosecuting Attorney has just called him a "killer" moments before. This is his time to take the stand and tell his side. He knows, however, that the jury is set to find him guilty no matter what he says.

Pick your eyelines so that you can look from Prosecutor to Judge, and then to the group of Townspeople. He hates the Prosecutor. He respects and likes the Judge. The jurors and other townspeople watching are "simple folk" that are too weak to do his job, and too naïve to understand how he must kill bad people, so he is contemptuous of them all.

When he says his brother got a grave "out yonder", he's referring to the courthouse graveyard where criminals are buried.

Despite his fury, he still is ready to accept the process of law. "Hang me if you must" is his resignation to the idea that he will die for his belief in the system.

By Nautic Von Horn

DON'T BLOW IT

Man

Hey you! Look at me, look at me, right here in the mirror. No, there's no one else around, just me. Don't you recognize me? I'm you, from the future. I'm in the mirror. I'm real, though. I'm really here for you, from the future. Do I look that different? Wha—heavier? Sure, but you were a total fatty five years from your now. I've worked off most of that weight. Fat or not, you have a future, Bud. I'm telling you so you don't blow it.

This is the night, isn't it? She left that stupid note. Look, Bud, this is not the end of our world. We'll be all right. No, she never comes back. You can't get her back. She's gone. You feel like dying. You feel like the center of your being, the most meaningful part of you, your reason for living is lost, gone forever. I know!

Put the gun down. Eight billion people. Four billion of them women. You're a romantic; you think there was just one meant for you. But do you hear how silly that is? Believe me, you'll meet more. Bud, drop the gun!

Good boy. I'll see you later.

Oh, and you really don't need to eat so much.

NOTES:

Suicide is never an easy subject, nor should references to guns be lightly thrown about. While there is comedy in this bit (in the references to weight) you don't want to be overly flippant. Be deadly serious about your mission to come back in time to save yourself.

If you think about it, you must not have killed yourself in the past or of course there wouldn't be any "you" to come back and save yourself. But maybe you seriously injured yourself … something bad, and future you wants to prevent that from happening.

You've come from the future to talk some sense into your past self. Imagine you are looking at yourself in the mirror when your future self appears. Your future self must first spend time initially to convince you that you are you.

Then look for and see the note. You've come back to this certain time for a purpose. To save yourself. It was vitally important that you came back, and you accomplish your mission by getting old-you to drop the gun. "I'll see you later" has real meaning for you.

If you've ever lost in love, this one may call to you. Hopefully, you were never suicidal, but we've all felt like we'd "just rather die" at some point after losing a lover.

"Bud" can be a name or just a nickname. Change it if you want to use your own. And of course, change genders as may better fit you.

By Nautic Von Horn

I WANT YOU TO SEE

Lover

I want you to see something. I mean, hear something, actually. I wrote a poem. Just, just a minute, okay? It's short.

"Without the ocean, the beautiful beach is just a desert. The mighty ocean pounds on the beach, caresses the sands, again and again, rising and falling, a timeless embrace. And the beach takes it, loves it. What good is an ocean where waves circle the globe forever, never landing on a shore? Where waves build in intensity, but find no release? An ocean needs the land to define it, control it, measure it. To tame it."

Will you marry me? Oh, wait! There's another verse.

"An ocean can evaporate, dry up, leaving nothing but the impression of where it had been. But the sandy beach never dissolves away. Its tiny rocks may shift and ebb, but never disappear, locked in immortality. Cold and uncaring for the tumultuous sea."

Okay, that's it. What? You didn't like it?

NOTES:

Love is blind, and it makes fools of us all. This person is both head over heels in love and clueless.

The poem is horrible, of course. And worse, it has creepy overtones. But don't read the poem as if it's creepy; that impression will come anyway. You're in love, so be romantic.

You can cheat with this monologue. No need to memorize the poem. It's fine to read the poem, as that is likely what the person would do.

The person listening to this must be cringing by the end of the poem. The answer to the proposal is going to be "Hell no!" But the Lover doesn't expect that answer and is surprised at the end.

SHE NEVER SAID THAT

Man

Shut up! I don't care if you are a cop. Just shut the hell up!

I see what you're doing, you know. This is just more of that "good cop – bad cop" crap. She didn't say that about me. You're lying and you think I'm going to break, keeping me up all night with no sleep, asking the same questions all night long. Is it morning? Don't I get breakfast or something?

She never said that. Never. You made it up. She would never. I told you – we're getting married soon as her divorce is final. We'd be engaged right now if she could announce it publicly, but she can't, because of what that would do in her divorce. She'd lose millions. No one can know we're together. But I'm telling you, confidentially, so you understand: one more month, maybe two, tops. That's all I had to wait until the divorce is done. Two months! That's not enough reason to kill anyone. I can wait. So, I had no motive. Why would I throw it all away? Just two months!

No, no, she never said that. You lying piece of crap. Get the good cop back in here. Tell him I want a cup of coffee. Black.

NOTES:

The cops think this guy killed his girlfriend's husband. Maybe he did – what do you think?

One cop told him that she confessed. That she blamed the killing on him. That's what he is reacting to, refusing to believe that she said anything like that.

Whether guilty or not, he puts up a good defense. He knows about motives and tries to reason with the cop. He also tries to distract the cop with talk of breakfast and coffee.

Maybe he is an innocent boyfriend, in love and confident that he can wait another two months. He reacts with righteous anger, shocked to be accused. He reaches his breaking point and tells the cop to "Shut up!"

Or, maybe he's a hardened criminal who knows exactly how to handle an interrogation.

You choose.

By Nautic Von Horn

BOYS NEVER TALK

Man

Boys never talk. You know that, right? Not about meaningful stuff. Maybe the weather, or which team is best. Or the biggest fish. But never about feelings.

There was one time when I was 13 and me and my best friend, Doug, got in a deep conversation about why his parents liked me better than him. We were in a boat at the time, zipping full speed around a lake. It was a tough subject. He looked at me. And I looked at him. Like a real conversation. A rare moment for boys.

Then we realized suddenly that he was steering the boat right into the shore.

He turned, and we barely missed these huge sunken tree trunks that were in the shallows. We could have died.

We learned our lesson. No more deep conversations. They're dangerous.

NOTES:

This is tongue-in-cheek fun. Campy, even. Flippant.

Whereas most of these monologues can be done by anyone, this one is meant to be performed by a male actor. You could change the gender, I suppose, but everyone knows girls have no problem talking openly with each other!

While the guy is resolute in his determination that deep conversations are dangerous, there is a flip side to his emotions. He wishes it weren't so. He remembers fondly the one time when he and his friend did actually look each other in the eyes and have a meaningful conversation – or at least the start of one. He envies the easy way girls can talk with each other.

This piece works best for older actors, with enough age on them that it's a long look back to age 13. That memory of the one time is made more special because it was just once in a long life – it wouldn't be nearly as poignant if said by a 17-year-old.

By Nautic Von Horn

WE CAN'T VISIT MOMMY

Father

Ahem. Uh. Kids, we – we're not, uh – we're not going to the hospital to see Mommy this morning. Mommy's – Mommy's illness is – uh – it got worse last night and – uh – Sometimes people get sick and they don't get better. Sometimes they get worse. Sometimes – uh – We can't visit Mommy anymore.

But we're gonna have tuna casserole for dinner, just the way you like it, just like Mommy made. So, get ready. We're going to the store, OK? We need tuna and noodles. And root beer, OK. It's a special day. Anything else? Whoa, no junk food. OK, alright, but just a little, and just this once.

And, um – then on Saturday we're gonna have a party for Mommy. OK? Grandpa and Grandma are coming, and all your aunts and uncles, and we'll get all dressed up. You'll know lots of kids there. Your cousins – remember Craig and Sherrie? And Oscar? Oscar. The little fat kid you said rolled in the dirt and looked like a seal? Yeah! Remember? We're gonna have fun.

It'll be fun.

NOTES:

How can you tell young children that their mother died?

This father wants to be honest with his kids, but can't bring himself to say the words.

This is addressed to multiple young children. Young enough that they don't understand what he's tried to say. They get more excited about wanting root beer and junk food. And whether there will be kids to play with.

The loneliness of being a single father is here. He has to keep up a good front for his kids, but at the last line he loses it. Look away from the kids at that point – that line is not directed at them.

Note how the character's objective changes in each paragraph. First, he wants to tell his young children that their mother died. Second, he wants to be a good father, and help the children move on with a normal life. And third, he realizes he can't just move on because he has to prepare them for the funeral.

And then, finally, we see his own pain. The line "It'll be fun" is not addressed to the children. This is the father realizing what he just said, that the funeral would be fun, and truly internalizing that his wife died.

DON'T GOTTA GO

Dog

Hey, boss! Boss! Man, I wish you would listen. You never listen to me. I mean, you hear me, but you never really listen.

It's a nice day to be out here, and this is some beautiful grass that feels really good between the toes, but I don't gotta go.

I don't see you going. Why should I go?

I appreciate the slack in the leash – I really do – but I don't need to stop here. This is a big park. I'd rather be running around. Did you see the squirrels?!

And I appreciate your patience with me, but I don't gotta go. I'd know if I had to, wouldn't I? You think it's my time, and I know you have your schedules and plans and things to do, but I just don't gotta go.

Besides, I can go later on the carpet.

NOTES:

The clue that this is a dog speaking is right up front, when he says "Man, I wish you would listen." He's talking to his man. Of course, the audience figures out later that he is a dog – usually when he talks about his leash.

He feels lots of frustration, because he just wants to go play and thinks it stupid that his master is insisting on toilet time. But he can barely hold back his excitement at being in the park – feeling delightful grass and seeing SQUIRRELS!

Take a moment and "try" to go to the bathroom. I do this before the line about patience.

Then his emotion transitions to puppy-dog sadness, when he comes to accept that he won't be allowed to run after the squirrels.

And imagine the scorn he would feel talking about the silly things his master does for such things as human work and schedules.

The final line is, of course, comedic. He finds the perfect solution, with all the excitement and happiness a dog can bring.

ONE QUESTION

Rescuing Brother

No, I'm not a cop. Alright? You gotta get that
straight. You're hung up over due process,
Constitutional rights, and all the get-out-of-jail
cards that worked for you in the past, but none of
that is me. Alright? Now, you have a choice to –
Whoa, whoa, whoa! Sit down!

You think you're safe, hiding in this back room
with your goons out front. But they're gone. No,
that's not true, and I want us to be truthful. Your
goons are still out front, they're just not coming to
help you. The big one? The one with the hat? He's
out for a week, maybe more, and you're gonna
need to cover the hospital bills - presuming he
gets there. The other two, the short guys? You can
probably get them up in a day or two. Nothing
broken. Not really. Some dental work might be
nice, if you spring for that.

Point is they're not coming to save you. You got
no one. You got me. So now, you need to make the
right choice.

I'm gonna ask just once. And you're gonna tell me
exactly what I need to know. Because then I'll
leave you alone. But if you choose wrong, I'm
gonna burn this place down, right now, with you

sitting right there, crispy in that smelly old Naugahyde chair.

I'm not a cop. I'm Dora Robertson's brother! So ... where is she?!

NOTES:

This is a dark piece, but the warmth arises from realizing he's desperately searching for his sister. And he knows she was somehow involved in the local gangster's business.

This guy is not a criminal type; however, he has skills. He took care of the bodyguards, and is now fully capable of intimidating (or killing) the boss crook. Think of him as a tough military guy returning from overseas to find his sister in trouble.

There's nothing special about the name Dora Robertson. Feel free to use whatever name may sound best to you. Put the stress on "brother" as that revelation is more important than the name.

By Nautic Von Horn

DOC THIS ISN'T WORKING

Psychology Patient

Doc, this isn't working. You never say anything,
and I get that yeah it's supposed to be me talking –

Three tornadoes spinning wildly over a herd of
giraffes.

But every Wednesday for six months, that's a long
time; it seems by now you could say something
about my progress –

Oh, a million butterflies crossing a turbulent ocean.

Or lack thereof. Am I getting better? Am I healing?
Say something, Doc –

Amish girls or maybe Mennonite, Jewish,
whatever, on a two-horse buggy on a bumpy dirt
road. They're laughing at me.

You've helped me access my "inner eye", the power
of my imagination, and I get that that's good –

Elephants balancing on mushrooms.

Good for me, since I'm an actor, a screenwriter, and
imagination is vital to my success –

Eww, my god. A submarine sunk at the bottom with all hands screaming their last breaths as they drown, clawing at the steel hatches, their fingernails ripping out. Ughh.

I can look at these ink squirts and let my subconscious thoughts come out, but Doc, I'm not making any real headway here.

Mmmmm, three trays of chocolate chip cookies, steaming, coming right out of the oven in Grandma's oven mitts.

I think it's time to stop. I mean, thanks, you're great, this has been fun, but I – what? The last six cards were all the same image? That's something. Well, I'll be back next Wednesday.

NOTES:

Pick a spot where you "see" the ink squirt cards. The conversation with the doctor should then be on a different eye line, either as if you are looking at the doctor or just elsewhere.

In the conversation you are struggling with how to tell the doctor you're quitting. It's a break up. But let yourself go with each of the ink squirt cards, especially the last ones. Pick different emotions. For example: awe (three tornadoes), joy (million butterflies), suspicion (Amish girls), amusement (elephants), terror (submarine), and peace (cookies).

By Nautic Von Horn

TRYING TO REMEMBER YOUR NAME

Ex-Spouse

Wow. Hi. I was trying to remember your name the other day.

The first year after our divorce I was a wreck. Mental case. Couldn't sleep unless I had Peter Gabriel playing all night in my headphones.

The next few years weren't much better. I worked a lot. Eventually married an alcoholic, had two kids, divorced the alcoholic.

Over the years I'd think of you now and then, whenever something reminded me of you. That was every day, at first. Every shadow, every sound, every taste. Then just rare moments. Like hearing our song, Queen's "You're My Best Friend."

But last week I realized I was finally over you. I saw your profile picture on the school reunion site and for a moment I was like, who's that? Isn't that amazing? Who's that.

And now, here you are. Aren't reunions fun?

NOTES:

Reunions suck, IMHO. There are some people one works hard to forget, and then seeing them later can be very jarring. Especially if that person is an ex-spouse.

What's going on here? You choose. Maybe the end is sarcastic, because seeing the ex-spouse is horrible. OR maybe the end is straight up, and now that they've met again they can re-establish their friendship / relationship. Who knows?

SO YOU'RE A WRITER

Fan

You're a writer, huh? What do you write? Would I have seen anything you did? Doesn't matter, never mind. I got an idea for a book that would make a great movie. You write it and I'll split the royalties, huh?

Listen, there's never been such a good idea. Nothing like it so it's a guaranteed blockbuster. I'd write it myself 'cept I'm not a writer.

I'll tell it to you now, and you can put the commas in later, and all the other official boring stuff.

No, wait, don't go anywhere. This will take a few minutes. You don't want to miss a word. Just hold on, they're not boarding your flight yet, and anyway there's always another flight later to wherever you're going. Come on, you can buy me a beer and I'll tell you the whole thing. Oh, well, I could go with you then - do you know if the flight is sold out? If you get me a ticket I'll sit next to you.

Wait, come back. Come back. Can I get your email?

NOTES:

This one makes me think of Monty Python, but I can't explain why.

The Fan is clearly clueless. He doesn't realize how belittling he is to the writer, and doesn't recognize that the writer urgently wants to get away.

It's all about him. He knows, down deep, that his idea is good, so he doesn't entertain the slightest doubt about whether other people will like it. And therefore can't understand why the writer would walk away from making millions on a sure bet.

By Nautic Von Horn

I QUIT

Executive

You can tell me. I won't tell anyone else. You know I can keep a secret.

Do I need to update my resume? Should I be looking? You'd tell me, right?

I know you don't want to start a stampede for the door, rats jumping off a sinking ship and all that, but a lot of people say you're selling the business. I mean people are talking - not me, I'm not the kind to spread rumors, but everyone - well, I heard it in accounting. You know how Richard talks. But I'm sure he only told a few of us. He only told me and a couple other execs - and the execs should know, right? We haven't told any of the rank and file. Let's keep this at the top, eh?

So, if you're selling and we're losing our jobs I'd appreciate a heads up. Who's the buyer? Ah, come on, I know there's a buyer. Of course, you have to say it's a rumor - I get it. But tell me. Just whisper. I've been working for you since the beginning. I've been a loyal employee. As long as we've been together, how can you keep it a secret from me?

Seriously? You're not going to tell me? Me? Well, hell. You know what? I quit.

NOTES:

Loyalty isn't what it used to be in the workforce. Still, you hope your boss would be kind enough to warn you if the company was being sold and you might soon be out of a job.

At least, this person thinks so. She's listened to the rumors of a pending sale and bought into her fears so much that she refuses to take her employer's word that it's just a rumor. It becomes a self-fulfilling prophesy, when she quits (loses her job) over her fears of losing her job.

Is this person paranoid? I wouldn't say so. She thinks it's just fine and normal for the executives of a company to withhold information from the lower-level employees – and she's suspicious that information is now being withheld from her. She's afraid.

Her anger develops from believing she has a right to know. She's an "executive" and "loyal" and has been there since the beginning of the company. She may even consider her boss to be a friend, and not just a co-worker. Which leads to her "how dare you" type reaction at the end.

HERE FOR THE JOB

Applicant

Hi. Yes, here for the job. They sent me up to talk with you.

I guess you're "the man," huh? Not to say you have to be the "man" of course. You could be a woman. I mean you could have been a woman. "The woman." Not that you identify as a woman. That's not what I mean. I mean, you could, of course. Nothing wrong with that. Man - woman, it's hard to tell today. Oh, you look like a man, of course you do. Broad shoulders, manly chin. A man's man, what? Chiseled face, good solid physique. No one would think you're feminine. I'm - uh - by the way, I'm not gay. That all sounded a bit gay, huh? But I'm not homophobic either. I'm not against anyone being gay. Of course not. So, if you are -- uh, hey, do you want my resume? My cell phone number's on it. Oops, that sounds like I'm hitting on you now, doesn't it, when I never would. Not that you aren't –

Oh, hell. Just forget it.

NOTES:

Comedy is pain.

This poor man. He wants so badly to be hired, and he's eager to say anything that will help him in the interview. Too eager.

This would be a perfect piece for George Castanza (Jason Alexander's character on *Friends*). Or Basil Faulty (Cleese's character on *Faulty Towers*). The bumbler who tries hard to succeed but puts his foot in his mouth every time.

Comedy great Jack Lemon advised actors to never play for the comedy. Play it straight and let the comedy just happen. Do your best to keep a straight face with this one. Play it as if your character wants only to get the job, not a laugh.

By Nautic Von Horn

JULIE JULES

Aunt

Hey Jul -- Jules. I'll try, okay? I'll keep apologizing every time I get it wrong, but I'm probably going to keep messing up.

You've been my "Niece Julie" for 15 years. I saw you the day you came from the hospital all wrapped up in pink, with the cutest pink bow taped to your head since there wasn't enough hair for a bow. And, not to be too graphically insensitive, but I saw you -- you know, all of you, at diaper changes. And you're all girl. No question, I remember.

Christmas and birthday times we gave you dresses, ballet tutus, skirts. Sure, you can still wear those or whatever, but it's hard to remember you're a boy now. Jules is a good name, but I'm going to slip and call you Julie now and then by mistake. "Nephew Jules" ... I'll try.

But Jules, I don't know how I can refer to you as "they". There's only one of you. Yeah, I'm sorry, I just don't get it. But I'm trying, Jules, I'm trying.

NOTES:

Aunt, uncle, or whatever other family relationship you prefer to use. This character is a bit older. At least old enough to have a relative who they've seen grow up from a baby.

This character is not as "woke" or "hip" as some. She is struggling to adapt to the modern world, not because of any animosity toward any particular people, but simply because she feels the world doesn't make as much sense as it used to. She's stuck fighting the logic of how a single person could ever be referred to as "they" since that seems to indicate plurality. (Of course, we've always used "they" for an individual in certain grammatical sentences – for example, "Give your paper to the teacher when they're ready for it.")

Yet love prevails. This character loves and supports Jules and wants to do everything they can to make Jules happy.

Love, confusion, embarrassment, fortitude, and whatever other emotions you divine – make sure to put them all in there for this heartfelt piece.

HERE WE GO FOLKS

Doctor

Okay, folks! I'm here. The moment we've all been waiting for. Let's do it.

Hi, Dad, good to see you. Just step over there out of the way, will you? Little more. Yeah, stay back there.

Darla, is that you under that mask? You sneaky little minx. I haven't seen you for weeks.

Hello, Julie. You're looking good. We're still on for dinner tonight, right? Mmmm, I can't wait.

And of course the star of the show. Hello, dear. How are you? No, don't try to talk. Listen, Mom, I can see you're ready. You're just about there. Just another minute or so. And I have a very special dinner date to get to, so I'm going to count to three and you know what to do, right? Yes, of course you do!

Okay, everybody. Darla, you catch. One, two, three. Push!

Oops. Darla, where were you?

NOTES:

Comedy again, almost slapstick. I think of Alan Alda's doctor character in *M.A.S.H.* The same glib womanizing type.

He waits to come in until the woman is fully dilated and ready to give birth. No doubt, he was watching tv, playing cards, or maybe even off drinking somewhere until getting called in.

This is a doctor who doesn't care much about his patients. He tells the father to stay back, and then treats the mother as a thing more than a human. Not the nicest guy, huh?

You choose how nice. Go for comedy, maybe. Or, if you want to make it darker, consider adding another line at the end: "Oh, yuck. That'll cost me in malpractice, won't it?"

SO SORRY SIR

Waiter

No, sir. I promise you, this is not just the same drink you didn't like. I took that drink back to the bartender and she remade it for you. Again. Third time's a charm, perhaps.

No, really. It just looks like the same glass. We have many of them at the bar, just like this. Would you like to try the drink now, sir?

I can't take it back when you haven't even tried it. It's not the same glass. A similar smudge perhaps, but not the same. Many of our glasses have smudges like this, I'm sure.

Sir, I can't, not until you try the drink. Here. Just take it, sir. If you don't like it, then I'll replace it, again. But how can I tell the bartender to remake it when you haven't even tried the drink? I can't tell her the smudge looks threatening! Sir, just a sip. Here, just, just take a sip –

Oops. So sorry, sir.

NOTES:

If you've ever waited tables you might relate to the desire to dump a drink in someone's lap. Dealing with the public is the hardest part of working in restaurants. Always having to stay polite and treating the customer as if they are right, no matter how unreasonable they may be.

This waiter has made multiple trips between the bar and this customer, who has complained repeatedly that the drink was not correct. Now the waiter is bringing the drink back for the third time, after having made sure that the bartender got it right. And now the customer has the nerve to say that it looks like the same glass he just refused!

The waiter keeps calm, mostly. Some snide comments, such as that there are many glasses behind the bar, but that's as far as one may go with the customer.

When the customer wants to reject the drink yet again and have it remade, without even tasting it, the waiter starts to lose patience and gets flustered.

Is spilling the drink an accident? You choose.

Is the waiter really apologetic at the end, or sarcastic? You choose.

By Nautic Von Horn

I'M LATE FOR BREAKFAST

Cop

Well? How are we doing in here? Hmmm?

Oh, mister. The tight mouth approach is not your best bet. Look where it got you last night. Why don't you talk to me. We can start with your name. What's your name? What's your first name? Give me something to call you.

Okay, mister. If that's your game stay quiet. The boys dragged you in just after midnight so we don't have to put you in front of a judge until tomorrow morning. Twenty-four hours plus. There's water there in that toilet, but I'm afraid there's no food for anonymous guests. And no phone calls to lawyers either. Not 'til you identify yourself and tell us why the money wasn't with the gun. Oh, yeah. We found the gun, with your prints.

You know, if you were to tell me where you hid the money, maybe you and I could work a deal.

No? Well, maybe this afternoon then. Excuse me. I'm late for breakfast.

NOTES:

A cop checks on a suspect in jail.

A gun is mentioned, and prints on the gun, and missing money, so we can infer that the suspect is likely guilty of something. But is the cop good or bad? Is he offering to help the suspect in return for getting his hands on the missing money? Play it either way.

Police departments often have laws they must follow regarding how long they can keep someone for questioning. In this story, the police must bring a suspect before a judge within 24 hours of booking them for arrest. I know for a fact that the police in some jurisdictions will routinely hold prisoners in police cars and delay getting them to the jail until Midnight, so that the suspect is booked on the next day's paperwork and they are not required to take the suspect into Court that morning. Whether that is a widespread practice or not, the process in this monologue is certainly not fictional.

Whether the suspect would be held with just toilet water to drink, and not allowed a phone call prior to divulging his name probably does surpass reality. But hey, that's what this cop does; maybe there are less modern police departments where this could happen. Or call it poetic license on my part, or perhaps it's proof that this is a dirty cop looking to score the money for himself. Again, play it either way.

The cop is clearly aware of the suspect's thirst and hunger. That's his leverage. Play it up.

By Nautic Von Horn

NOT IN MY KITCHEN

Cook

Please don't misunderstand me. This is your house, and I am honored to be included in the staff. I have served your family happily, starting with your parents at the main lodge twenty-one years ago, and next month will be six years with you.

I keep your kitchen in strict conformity with your dietary instructions, as communicated to me both by you yourself and by the doctor you had tour the kitchen facilities three years ago. All this I have done, if you will allow me this moment to speak openly, Ma'am, to the utmost of my abilities and indeed to a certain level of perfection I can take pride in -- performance which, while you rarely praise my dishes, has garnered no complaints from you.

Hence my shock upon learning this morning that your husband's Cigar Club intends Friday next to take over the kitchen in its entirety to soak tobacco leaves in the sinks, to defile the cutting boards with the juice of tobacco leaves, in order to wrap something called cigarillos.

Madam. I appeal to your sensibilities. I find there is but one thing more I can say clearly. Not in my kitchen!

NOTES:

Cook is shocked, but remains in control. Until the end, that is. "Not in my kitchen!" takes backbone. She speaks out against her employer, which is contrary to all her training, background, and culture. This is a huge moment for her which she has to build up to, force herself to speak out in this manner.

Cook begins properly deferential and respectful, which she sees as her place as part of the household service staff. She's proud of her long service with this family. You may think of this as a period piece, although in modern times this type of pride in service (not slavery!) still continues.

But the kitchen is her responsibility, and the idea of the Cigar Club taking over is just too much. The proverbial straw breaking the camel's back. She is drawing a line and objecting strongly, so strongly in fact that she is prepared to quit if the madam of the house does not take her side in this.

Be sure to find the horror in the mere idea that something called a "Cigar Club" would be allowed into her kitchen!

OPENING NIGHT

Ticket Taker

Shh! Look, I can let you in free tomorrow night, or come back any night next week, but not tonight. I'd get fired. This is opening night and everyone's here. I mean, everyone. The director's watching me like a hawk. Get out of here before you get me in trouble. Why'd you come on opening night?

That's not fair, you work at a movie theater. It's not the same at a stage. Yeah, you let me in twice last week. I said thanks, didn't I? I appreciated it. But come on, those movies had been playing for weeks already. Hell, the theaters were barely half full. And the popcorn was stale. You need to tell someone about the popcorn. That's the first sign of a place going out of business, soon as the popcorn sucks.

Of course, we're friends, best friends. Oh no, don't give me that guilt trip. I'm going to get fired!

Oh, alright, sheesh. Stop. You know I can't stand those big eyes. Quick, get in. But if you get caught, you don't know me!

NOTES:

Growing up in San Diego I developed a network of friends at different theatres, and could get in free to see just about any show. That is, unless it was opening night. The opening is almost always packed, with theatre critics and everyone the director especially invited to attend. That night is such a big deal that it's not likely at all anyone like me could slip in for free.

These are good friends, maybe even roommates. They frequently help each other get into shows for free. They have history. Which is why the guilt trip works. Those big puppy-dog eyes get to the ticket taker.

Popcorn is obviously very important to the ticket taker. They're convinced that bad popcorn is a sure indication of the movie theater's pending closure, and that it's important to warn the friend. It's a bit of comic relief here, but don't throw that passage away because the ticket taker is trying to help the friend.

ACTION!

Director

"Action! Action!" That's my line. That's what I get to say! Not you. I hired you to be my first AD – that's "assistant" director, not director! You understand me? I get to say "Action!" Just me! Only me.

You think you want to direct, but you don't know a thing about directing. Let me tell you where you're going wrong.

Movies are made when they're written and when they're edited in post-production. Not on the day they're filmed, not when they're acted. All of this you're doing is just the junk that I have to sort through when we edit, and I delete 99%! 99% of what you do, your playtime with the actors and all your camera toys. And no, I am not drunk when I edit!

So, you keep doing you. Go ahead, run the set. Get the cameras, microphones, lights, the stars, the props. You get it all ready for me. Then I come in and I yell "Action!" Not you! Yelling "Action" is my job and I can do it very well, sir.

Now, get over there and get me ready.

"Cut!"

NOTES:

Believe it or not, there are some directors who believe that the actual filming days are not important, because the movie is put together in the editing process. They don't care much about the actors' performance or anything else about the filming process, because they trust that literally anything can be "fixed in post." (I cringe when working anywhere near this type of director.)

On top of such belief, this director is drunk. Which makes them totally unreasonable – there's no point in anyone trying to talk to them at this point.

Being able to call "Action" and "Cut" is the essence of the director's position, according to this director, and he is prepared to let the 1AD do absolutely everything else so long as he still gets the respect of being a director. When the 1AD called "Action" himself, that was tantamount to a mutiny. Hence the director's raging response.

NEW SLAVE

Teenage Girl

We're going to be good friends. Sisters have to be.
When your mom marries my dad, that'll make
you my little sister. And me the big sister.

So, let's get things straight right away. You're my
slave. You do everything I say, or else you'll be in
big trouble. My high school days and nights are
going to get real busy as soon as I can start car
dating, and I won't have time for chores around
the house anymore. That's going to be all you
now. Got it?

And this is our sister secret. Don't be telling your
mom, you hear me? If they have more kids, the
next one can be your slave, but you're mine.
That's how it works.

Now, if you do a really good job and never tell,
I'll give you a dollar from my allowance. Oh, I
don't know if you'll get your own allowance --
actually you know, I remember, when I was your
age I didn't so you won't either. Just forget about
that. Don't even ask for an allowance cuz they'll
just say no until you're old like me.

Oh, I love you so much! We're sisters!

NOTES:

      With sisters like this, who needs ... brothers? Siblings can be the worst enemies growing up!

      This sister isn't evil. She's just protecting her home turf, making sure that the little one coming in understands right off who's boss. It's a control thing. Establishing the pecking order right away.

      She's thrilled to have a sister. She's been an only child, and the thought of having a sibling is wonderful, in addition to being scary.

      Having a new sister will be wonderful, but only so long as she sets the rules. To her, having a new sister means she will be able to enjoy new freedoms – such as having more time for boys because she can duck her chores.

      And a $1 bribe seems like a perfect inspiration to seal the deal ... that is, until the new sis asks if she will get her own allowance. She has to scramble a bit.

      But then comes back to the idea of how wonderful this will be.

MAN AT BAR

Man

It's crowded in here. I said, it's crowded in here!

You're kidding, the blonde? The tall one? She said that? Oh boy. Okay. Wow. Maybe this is it. I've been divorced long enough. Maybe I deserve this. How do I look? Okay. Hold my beer. I'm going in. I can do this.

Wait, what? You were kidding? George! What the hell? That's not funny! You get to go home every night to Julia. I got a tv.

It's not funny! You know, maybe we should stop coming here. How am I ever going to find someone with friends like you? I'm not sure we can be friends anymore. You're always pulling pranks on me. It's not funny, George!

You're kidding, the brunette?

NOTES:

Total goof ball.

This guy is such an easy mark for his friend to prank. But he's a decent guy, fun to have a beer with.

Plenty of opportunity here for some movement. He needs to react to what his friend is saying (with the "You're kidding" both times), and then look around to see where his friend is indicating, and which blonde. Then also as he works himself up to go over to talk with her. Also in his reaction to realizing George pranked him again. I would play this very physically, especially keeping in mind that they are in a bar where conversation is hard to hear.

The ending is sweet and simple. Despite all his protests about George's cruelty, he falls for the same gag again. Hook line and sinker. Never even imagining that George did it again.

ROCKY'S DOG

Stallone

Come on, you're kidding, right? You won't sell him back to me? Look, when I sold him to you, I told you I'd want him back, like, you know, when I got money. I got money now. I sold a script.

Yeah, they paid me good money for my story about a boxer who wins against all odds. They're gonna make it a movie. You can see it in a couple years. You'll like it. Anyway, I really want my dog back. You paid me forty dollars. I'll give that back, plus interest. Let's call it a hundred bucks. How bout it? Double your money and more.

Sure he's a great dog, but you haven't had him long enough to fall in love with, not like me. Butkus and I were together for a long time, since he was a puppy. He's like a brother to me. Five hundred, huh? Come on, man. Five hundred dollars for a dog that cost you forty!

Look, alright, what do you want? He's my brother. I never should have sold him, but I had to. Now I got money, so what do you want?

What? Fifteen thousand! Are you crazy? You can ask that for a dog? You know, fine. Just give me my dog.

NOTES:

This is based on a supposedly true story, that Sylvester Stallone was once so poor that he had to sell his dog. The amount varies but something like $40 or $50. And then later he bought his dog back, after selling the script for *Rocky*. But he had to pay thousands to get the dog back (again, the amount varies in different stories).

Of course, this is just how I imagined the conversation may have gone.

That dog, by the way, is Rocky's dog in the first two movies. Such a lovable creature! It's no wonder Stallone fought to get him back.

(This whole story might be a totally false rumor. If any of you readers know whether it's true, or based on true events, I'd love to hear from you.)

By Nautic Von Horn

DAD WANTS YOU

Boy

I don't know anything. Nothing at all about that, or anything like it. I'd tell you if I did, Dad. Really.

Yeah, I was here. I was going to go up and do my homework but I didn't have much to do anyway, in fact I did most of it at school, actually all of it. And the trash was already taken out. So I was laying on the couch watching tv. In the family room, where the tv is, and the couch.

So I was facing the tv, not the kitchen. I couldn't see who was in there. Or hear. The tv was loud, cuz it was Mission Impossible and I like it loud. No way for me to see or hear anything that happened in the kitchen.

No, when it happened I was alone, watching tv. Mike? Uh, he wasn't with me when it happened. I was alone in the family room. I was just watching tv.

What? How do I know when it happened? Well, it happened, and later I saw the mess. And Mike? When I saw it he was watching tv in the family room. So anyway, I just went back to watching Mission Impossible. And then you came home.

All right. Mike! Dad wants you!

NOTES:

Oh, how we lied to our parents when we were kids! This boy is choosing his words carefully, in order not to tattle on his brother. But Dad sees through it.

He starts off with the general "know nothing" and only reluctantly admits that he was in the area.

The change comes when he get caught knowing exactly when the mess occurred. He realizes he's just thrown his brother under the bus, by saying that Mike was not in the living room watching tv when the mess happened but he was watching tv when the boy saw the mess – the implication being Mike made the mess and then went to watch tv.

"All right" is the boy's surrender. Then does he turn and call for Mike in glee, that his brother got caught even without his tattling to Dad? Or does he sound apologetic and worried that Mike is going to blame him? You decide.

By Nautic Von Horn

WITH YOUR PANTIES

Woman

Excuse me. Hi. I was over there -- oh, yeah, you saw me. That was dumb. I had that washer before you, but then I was waiting for my dryer to finish and I saw you come in and start your wash using the same washer. And then right before my dryer finished I saw you move your clothes over to a dryer.

Not that I was watching you really -- it's just that there aren't many people in here today.

Then my dryer buzzed and I was folding my clothes. Over there. That's my stack. I'm almost done.

Anyway, uh, I'm missing one thing and, uh, I think maybe it stuck to the inside of the washer. You know, I didn't see it. But the washer's empty now. So, uh, I think, uh, one of my pairs of panties is probably tumbling around with your boxers right now. Uh, could we -- or maybe when your dryer stops -- or, uh, I could give you my phone number.

Uh, hi. I'm Julie.

NOTES:

Perhaps the most awkward pick-up line ever.

This poor woman is smitten. She was just doing her laundry when in walked an incredibly hunky man. Of course she watched him, covertly. Fantasized about meeting him, but she is too shy to just go for a chat.

Then the horror of realizing her underwear must be in the dryer with the hunk's clothes!

By Nautic Von Horn

IT'S A TIMEX

Man

Ma'am, I repair old clocks, with brass movements inside. Seth Thomas, Howard Miller, Ridgeway, and a lot of the older clocks made before there were brand names. The first hall clocks - what you would call grandfather clocks - were invented in the 1600's. Carefully cut handmade gears. Wooden cases that ought to be in museums. Some of them are exquisitely beautiful, inside and out, with graceful lines, delicate hands, the sweetest details that make you want to simultaneously cry and sing. You can't manhandle such works of art. I have to caress them, touch them so gently, in order to coax them back to life again.

But ma'am, I'm a little confused. I told you on the phone I only do house calls for the large clocks that are hard to move. That clock next to your bed is a Timex. Not an antique. I'm afraid I'm still going to have to charge you the Sixty Dollar travel fee.

Ma'am? Why are taking off your clothes?

NOTES:

Repairing old clocks is a dying art. Good chance he's older.

He's poetic, too. The way he goes on about the beauty of clocks must have really excited his customer. No doubt he was poetic like that on the phone, too, and that's why she had him come over for a house call. His sensual imagery, the sweet and loving way he talks, how he has to caress them gently and coax them to life – ah, words that could charm almost any lovesick woman.

Is the guy clueless at the end? Or might he be amused at her approach and quite willing to see what happens next?

By Nautic Von Horn

I'LL TAKE TWO MORE

Customer

Hi, just the two shirts, please.

Wait, how much? $3.25? Ha, right. Seriously? For two Polo shirts? I mean, I know they're on sale and everything, but, uh, I think you made a mistake.

It can't be $3.25 for two brand new Polo shirts. I can see that's what your register says, but does that sound right to you? The sign said one shirt was on sale for $14.99. Fifteen bucks, times two that's thirty bucks. And then there's always tax, right? So ... you probably just got the decimal place wrong, and I don't want to take advantage --

No, I'm sorry. I'm not saying you did anything wrong. But your machine did. I'd feel bad if there's a mistake. It should be $32.50, right?

Seriously? $3.25? Computers never make mistakes? Right. Well, then.

Hey, you know what - hold on, I'm going to get two more.

NOTES:

Before you say that no cashier could ever be this stupid, please understand that this actually happened to me. I don't know if the teenager behind the counter was stupidly unable to understand, or if he was for whatever reason trying to cheat his company, but … it happened.

The customer has morals and wants to do the right thing. He goes to extra efforts to get the cashier to see the mistake and correct it. He tries hard, because otherwise it seems like stealing. Taking advantage of a simple mistake is as bad, in his mind, as if he shoplifted.

However, his morals only go so far. Ultimately, he realizes the cashier is not going to change the price, which means he will get two brand new shirts for only $3.25. And then – with an air of "if you can't beat 'em, join 'em" – he totally pushes his morals aside and doubles up.

And in his mind, he can justify this apparent theft in response to what the cashier said, that "computer's never make mistakes." Oh, yeah? Really?

HE RUNS KIND OF FUNNY

Father

Calm down, both of you! You're behaving like hyenas. Both of you. Young man, stifle yourself. This is no way to act in front of a lady. And you, daughter. That's no way to act as a lady.

Now, let's just talk this out and see what the problem is. Why are you coming back so early before curfew? And why are you standing out here on the front porch in front of God and everybody making so much caterwauling noise? If you can speak civilly now, tell me what happened.

Hold on, hold on! Don't both of you talk at once! All I hear is wallet this, and wallet that. What? Now, you wait a minute young man; there's no need I'm sure to get the police involved. And how dare you suggest my daughter is a thief? I think I've heard quite enough out of you. Run along, before I take a belt to your behind. You just get going, go home, you hear? And, maybe, don't come back. That's right, keep running!

He runs kind of funny, don't he? So, how much was in the wallet?

NOTES:

Hey, girls: is this the best dad ever, or what? A father should always take his child's side of any argument.

This father knows his daughter very well. He has no problem imagining that she stole money out of the boy's wallet. In fact, he sees no problem in that at all. Heck, he's even proud of her. If she can steal it, then he can help her run the guy off. They make a great team.

At first, he is just upset at the noise that has disturbed his quiet time. He's amused, too, at the childish behavior.

But then he reacts strongly to the idea of police involvement. That is certainly not what he wants, so he tells the boy to get lost. Notice, however, that he does take his cue from the daughter, too, when he says "maybe" don't come back – he's checking with her to be sure she doesn't want to see him again. And at her response he continues with "That's right, keep running!"

What a dad. Do you suppose he next asks her for a cut of the take?

By Nautic Von Horn

I DO PUZZLES

Sleuth

Puzzles? Oh, yes, I do puzzles. Crosswords, jumbles, word searches. Don't scoff; it keeps the little gray cells active. Even better are number puzzles like sudoku, because they teach us to see patterns, and it is the patterns in life that tell the most important stories.

You laugh, so be it. I realize to many of you I am an eccentric weirdo who doesn't belong on a crime scene. Despite the many times my deductions have solved your cases for you. Eh. You may laugh; it is free.

But while you all diligently go about collecting evidence, carefully photographing every bit of refuse at the scene, and labeling hundreds of cute little evidence baggies that you will store forever in box after box in your carefully guarded warehouses, who here sees what it means that the car keys are so far from the body? Hmmmm? Just as I thought.

Sudoku, people.

NOTES:

Think Sherlock Holmes. A brilliant but totally off-beat character.

Yes, he's a human calculator, able to see patterns that no regular mortal would ever suspect. But he is human. And he's feeling pain.

It hurts him deeply that he doesn't get the recognition he craves from all of the licensed crime experts. He's not a detective, he's not on the force officially, but he feels like he is every bit as good – and actually much better – and therefore there should be no scorn, or raised eyebrows, or smug comments, or anything of the sort aimed at him.

Not only should they not treat him like a freak, but he thinks they should be constantly praising him. He deserves accolades. He thinks he should be given gold medals for his successes.

By Nautic Von Horn

I'LL LEAVE NOW

Church Group Member

Father, I -- do I have to answer that? I'd rather not. Do I have to?

I love this group. I love all of you. For two years I've been coming most Tuesday and Thursday nights for the fun card games, darts, great conversation with really neat people. I've volunteered for bake sales and other fund raisers. I've brought more covered dishes to our potlucks than I can remember – I even cleaned the rectory attic with Bill and Joe. And you, Martha. I feel like I belong in this group, like I'm truly one of you. You're my family.

But, Father -- No one's ever noticed before, Father, until you. No one's ever asked me why I don't come to church on Sundays. It's a big crowd. I guess no one ever missed me.

Father, I don't want to lose my friends, but I can't lie to you, either.

I ... I don't believe in God.

Ok, I'll leave now.

NOTES:

Have you heard it said that "There are no atheists in fox holes"? That's the idea that people believe in a god when they are at risk of harm. But it is (perhaps surprisingly) true that there are many atheists in churches. People that are there for the comfort, the friendship, the feelings of belonging in a family. Tribalism can be a powerful enticement.

Imagine how you would feel if you were in a large church group and yet didn't share the stated religious beliefs of the group. Would you be afraid of getting "outed" from the group when your lack of belief becomes known?

If you are in the "in group" then you are accepted, even loved. But as soon as you are "other" then you are not in the group, not loved, and maybe even hated. The group would likely kick you out, prohibit you from participating in all the fun things you really enjoy doing.

This person is terrified. But this person is also, now that the matter has come to a head, not willing to compromise their principles. Not willing to lie. Not willing to hide anymore.

Think about how hard it is for someone who used to believe to actually finally say out loud words like "I don't believe in God." Not only the fear of losing friends, but there's also the inner doubt still: what if God does exist and He will strike me down for saying this? It is incredibly hard, almost impossible, for this person to speak these words.

By Nautic Von Horn

SOFT BUT NOT TOO

Spouse

Over here, let's try this one. Ooooh, so soft. Mmmmm. Uh-oh. Nope. Too soft. I'd fall asleep in the middle of all my programs.

Maybe this one? Ugh, no. That one? You're crazy. It looks like your mother's living room set and you are way too young to be turning already into your mother. I don't need two mothers-in-law!

Ok, here. Now, this is a chair! What do you mean its arms are poofy? I like big poofy arms. Like your arms. Whoa, jeez. Okay, okay, we don't need a divorce chair. Sheesh.

You like that one? Let me try it. Hmmm. Maybe. It does match our sofa. I don't know. I'd have to sit here a while. Maybe you should go get a Starbucks. Here's your chance to get that half chi mocha that I don't like the smell of, and I'll have time to try this chair. Actually, what I need is to watch tv and sleep in it, but how can I do that here? They don't make these display floors very user friendly. I know, go ask the guy if their return policy covers the delivery charge. And make sure their drivers use foot covers.

Mmmmmmmm. Soft, but not too. Yes, this might be my new chair.

NOTES:

Channel your inner Sheldon with this one. It is super important to some people to have just the right chair for tv watching and reading.

This person is totally obsessed with finding the right chair. So much so that they don't treat their spouse very nicely. They don't care about the salespeople or anything else. The only thing that matters is getting just the right chair.

By Nautic Von Horn

ZAP!

Father

I'm glad you're helping me, son. Just come up a couple steps on this ladder, so you can see better. Does your mom know you're in here? Well, maybe don't tell her. She worries too much.

Every man needs to know how to use tools and fix things around the house. This ceiling fan will be great on hot days. It'll increase the value of our house, too. Your Mom said we should call an electrician. Bah! Electricity is dangerous, but wiring is something every man should know. And when you know what you're doing, it's plenty safe. You just watch your old dad!

See these wires? The power comes in and the electrons make a circle through the fan, coming in one wire and going out the other. That's what runs the motor. You need two wires, white and black. This white wire on the fan connects to this white wire in the ceiling, like so. Of course, you have to turn the power off at the switch to be safe, before touching these ends. Some people even say you have to switch off the circuit breaker in the garage, but the wall switch is good enough to cut the electrical current.

So, next we put the black wires together, like so --

ARRRRRRRGH!

NOTES:

Here's your chance at physical comedy. We see it coming, of course, but that doesn't ruin the fun of the ending. Make it big. Don't hold back. Use gestures to show your son how to connect the white wires, and then reach for those black wires to set up the big shock.

By the way, you might be thinking that shutting off the switch would indeed cut the power to the fan, and therefore protect against shock. But many times, there are multiple wires running through an electrical box, such that turning it off at the switch does not guarantee there are no hot wires.

This father is proud of his abilities, wrong as his thinking is. He's showing off for his son, and also feels it important to train his son. On top of that, he is anxious to prove his wife wrong, that they didn't need to spend money on an electrician.

So, the ARRRGH is full of many emotions. Pain, too. He's surprised, angry, embarrassed, and humiliated. All that in one word.

By Nautic Von Horn

NOTHING THIS YEAR

Spouse

No, please, nothing this year. Don't do anything for my birthday. It's not a decade. It's nothing special and I don't need to celebrate the depressing fact that I'm getting older.

It is better though than the alternative. This side of the ground, right?

We've got other parties to focus on. You've got a big birthday coming next year. And the year after that is a milestone anniversary for us. So, let's just forget all about my birthday for the next few years.

Maybe you can just take me out for a nice dinner. Steak. A steak dinner and a show, a night out at some swanky little club. And I'd be wearing a new jacket, hint, hint. If you hurry, you could probably get good concert tickets. Say, would the Millers want to go with us?

I wonder what they'd get me. We could invite the Johnsons, too.

NOTES:

Comedy is fun, but remember Jack Lemon's advice: play the situation, not the comedy. Play it serious and the comedy will just happen.

This person is serious about not making a big deal out of the birthday. And equally serious about wanting steak dinner, a show, a new jacket, and presents from others, too. The hypocrisy is not recognized.

MR. NIGERIAN PRINCE

Phone Caller

My dear Mr. Nigerian Prince. So good to hear from you! I called you back as soon as I could, and I'm disappointed that you didn't pick up your phone, but I do so hope you get this message.

Imagine my grief to hear of your father, the king's passing. What a pickle you are in, having to find someone on such short notice that can help you inherit his fifteen million dollars. Please rest assured that I will happily help you relieve your burden. You mentioned my bank account, but of course in your grief you made a mistake. You don't need my bank account. Please send me the bank name and account number for your father's account, and we'll get this horrible burden transferred right away. You'll feel so much better, sire, without all that cash weighing on your mind.

May I say too, sire, that it was eminently wise of you to pick an unknown every-day-person like myself. Your father's ministers, lawyers, department heads, and accountants will never be able to find me. I am the perfect person to help you.

Do call soon.

NOTES:

Have you ever wanted to make this phone call?

Find the right balance between reverence and scorn. Of course, you don't really think the guy who called you is truly a prince or a king. Of course, you're just having fun calling him back. But it's fun to act as if he deserves to be called "sire" and the ridicule should be an underlying thread that isn't overly stated.

By Nautic Von Horn

CAN WE USE YOUR CAMERA?

Filmmaker

I'm making a new movie, and of course, I thought of you right away. We need you! There's plenty of good character roles that are perfect for you, brother. Take a look at our Facebook page and let me know what you want to audition for. You could probably even do more than one role, you're that good!

I know you want to act, but we also need crew -- do you still do that, too? Do you still have your sound mixing equipment, and those wireless lav mics? That'd be great if you'd bring those. Some LED lights, too, would be perfect.

It's a quasi-western, though the kind without horses cuz horses are way beyond our budget. Gonna be great, though! Who needs horses, right?

I hope you can join us. Let your friends know, will you? Such a big production, the more the merrier. By the way, I'm sending you our Gofundme link. Whatever you can throw in will be a huge help and we'll all love you for it. And I bet you can pass the link on to some of your millionaire friends, huh?

Hey, man. Good to see you again, brother. By the way, can we use your camera?

NOTES:

Do you have a friend like this? I have several, unfortunately. (I don't mind helping people, but too many times I feel like they're taking advantage of me.)

This is, however, told from the other side. You want to make a movie, but you don't have enough money for horses ... in fact, you don't have enough money for sound, lighting, or camera equipment, either. So, you need to sponge off of your "friends", even a "brother" you haven't seen for a long while.

The Entertainment World is full of people like this. Doesn't make them bad people. They're just hustlers, and sometimes the hustle is necessary to get things done.

Desperation is the key emotion here. This person really wants to make their movie, despite having no equipment and no money. Talking their friend into helping is the key to success.

By Nautic Von Horn

I COULD TIE THEM LAST WEEK

Spouse

Shit! I can almost ... Why do I have such long legs? No, get away! All right, I'm sorry, honey. I could tie them last week by myself, but they're so damn far away. I'm okay when I stick to the slip-on style like my fuzzy bunny-ear slippers. You sure I can't wear those today? I mean, it's just Walmart.

I'm going to start in the garden section today. From there to the milk and then back again. No quitting halfway. Not today. I feel great, better than last week. I know I'm kicking this damn cancer. When we do the next testing, you're going to see: everything's in remission. I feel it happening. I feel it.

I think it's just the medicine making me a bit dizzy, why I couldn't reach my shoes today. But honey, you were here, you're my savior. What would I do without you? When my cancer goes into remission that's going to be your success as well as mine, even more, all the things you do for me. You are my life, honey. Have I told you that recently? And you won't have to tie my damn shoes forever. I'll do it next week, you'll see.

NOTES:

Determination, frustration, anger, love – what else do you see in this one?

Starting off with frustration at failing to tie the damn shoes. Which becomes anger when the spouse tries to help, since that seems like pity and just points out the helplessness.

Love rules, however, and the anger is quickly swallowed. Followed by renewed determination to kick the cancer. Then back to love.

Isn't it wonderful to be an actor, imagining what fighting cancer may feel like? I hope you never experience it directly. Living vicariously as an actor is good enough for me!

By Nautic Von Horn

NO MORE SHEETS

Sibling

Do you believe in ghosts? I remember when we were kids dressing up for Halloween, in sheets with eye holes cut out. You always got more candy than me, and you'd say it was because you were a better ghost. But you just grabbed more.

Ghosts don't wear bed sheets. What the heck were we thinking? But now I know ghosts really are everywhere, all around us. I see them every day. I see them here in this room with us right now. Does that scare you? Maybe it should.

My kids and I were looking at old photos. Of course, most are long dead, but it's amazing how we look like those distant ancestors. My daughter looked at a picture of great grandma and said immediately, "It's Aunt Jill!" It did look just like you. We are our own ghosts. Walking, living ghosts, echoes of the past.

It's scary thinking how we end up like our parents. Did you know great grandma went crazy at age forty? You've got a year left.

But hey, it's not all bad. At least, we're not wearing sheets anymore.

NOTES:

Echoes in time. Family bloodlines can run true for many generations, good and bad.

Becoming like your parents can be a horrendous prospect for some. Truly scary.

This is typical sibling rivalry. Teasing. Jill may or may not look like great grandma, who may or may not have actually gone crazy. Have fun. Tease your sister.

TAKE A BREAK

Boyfriend

Can we go outside? Take a break, can you? I got to talk. Who cares if they fire you? They pay you shit, anyway. So, what if they hear me?

Good, come over here. No, wait. Let me talk. No, I can't talk at home. I just can't. Listen, stop interrupting. Let me say this now, while I can.

First, I love you. I do. But listen, honey, when you get home tonight I'm not going to be there. Shhhh, hold on. Nothing, you didn't do nothing. It's me, honey. It's me. Okay? I messed up. No, actually not me. Joe did. Yeah, you were right, okay? I didn't know how bad it was gonna get but listen, I gotta get out of here. I have to disappear. Have there been any cops in here tonight? Whew. But there will be. I told you, I messed up! Whatever, doesn't matter, and the less you know about it, you know?

Kim, we can't talk or see each other for a while. I took all the money out of our account so I can run. Kim! Stop thinking about yourself! I need it. It's the only way I can disappear. It was my money too. Jesus! Is that what's bothering you?! Kim, honey, honey, I'll pay you back, okay?

Someday. Someday, I will.

NOTES:

Love, fear, and desperation. The American saga.

Kim's boyfriend did something bad. And probably not for the first time. He seems only too familiar with the need to run and hide.

He starts out desperately needing to talk, and now. He makes enough of a fuss at Kim's work that she is forced to step out with him.

Kim of course wants to know what's happening, and you can imagine her interrupting throughout.

They live together, presumably boyfriend/girlfriend. Maybe married. They have a joint bank account. Kim knows what kind of guy she's with, and isn't terribly surprised that Joe got her man into trouble, but she is enraged to hear that her bank account has been raided.

He means it when he promises to pay her back. But … I wonder if he ever does?

By Nautic Von Horn

HAVE A COOKIE

Woman

Oh, there you are! My gosh, you have perfect timing. I baked some cookies today. Step inside. Can you smell them? Oatmeal chocolate chip. I hope you like them as much as the peanut butter cookies I made you last week. I mean the cookies I made last week, which you got when you delivered the hair dryer I ordered. Not that I made them for you, of course. Silly me.

Here, have a cookie. I already put some more in a box for you to put in your truck. This box waiting right here. Yes! See, I used the box you brought me last week, the hair dryer. You know, I ordered another one and it came by UPS, can you believe that? What a waste. No, uh, not a waste. I meant, um, that hair dryer didn't work so I sent it back. The good stuff comes Fed Ex.

Oh, that little computer thingee keeps track? Ha. Oh, my. Well, yes, you have brought me six of the same hair dryers in less than a month. I, uh, I have lots of friends and they make such good gifts. But what I need is a new crock pot; do you deliver those? I'm going to order that right now. By the way, I was planning on making some gingerbread cook --

What? A diet? You are kidding, I hope.

NOTES:

Oh, what a stud this Fed Ex driver must be!

As Jack Lemon said, play this straight. Don't go for the comedy. This woman has such a crush on the driver, and she fully believes the old saw, "The way to a man's heart is through his stomach."

And yet, she certainly doesn't want to seem desperate. She is, yes. Desperately in love. But must hold onto her dignity, too.

She never imagined the driver would know her order history, that she kept ordering hair dryers. Now, of course, she'll have to mix it up and order different things, so long as they all come by Fed Ex.

She slips repeatedly. First saying the cookies were baked for him, second that the order that came UPS was a waste, and then by getting caught ordering the same thing repeatedly (the one item she knew would come Fed Ex). She recovers nicely each time. However, the guy has likely caught on by the time he points out to her that his handheld computer tracks her purchases.

So, is the ending his rejection of her? Or is he really on a diet? How would she take it?

By Nautic Von Horn

JR. SCIENTIST

College Student

This is so cool! I can't believe I'm on this ship with you guys, doing marine biology research, and that I'm listed on the ship's log as "Junior Scientist"! Last week I was working in the university library; this week I'm "Junior Scientist." That's so cool! And you guys are exactly where I want to be career-wise in, like, 10 to 15 years, so I can learn so much from you!

Hmm, huh? You're studying the double-helix parasite that lives in the lower intestines of the San Bernadino flea that infests deep-water bi-valve molluscs off of Southern California. That's ... really specific. Oh, I understand. The days of Benjamin Franklin-type general science are ancient history. Now scientists have to find a niche. A specific, tiny, little subject to study.

Oh. And is that common? Both of you have to spend most of your time writing grant proposals, because if you run out of money you can't do any research at all? Wow. 90% of your time begging for money? And, then you research something maybe three people in the world care about. Wow. That's so ....

Uh, I'm thinking of changing my major to theatre. Wouldn't that be cool?

NOTES:

Total excitement followed quickly by complete disillusionment. Poor guy.

As a biology science major in college, he was already working in the science library and was lucky enough to get included in a research trip – the most exciting thing ever!

But the reality of science hits hard. He loves scientific subjects, especially marine biology, but his expectations are too romantic. He imagines himself studying the oceans like Jacques Cousteau used to, making great discoveries and telling the world about them. The idea that instead he would spend his entire career studying some little tiny something that basically no one would care about completely stuns him.

That his next thought is to change majors to theatre is an indication of his character. He wants (needs) a career that has more excitement and public acclaim. He goes from idolizing these scientists to scorning them, pitying them.

He wants to be cool. It hurts to think that his dream of becoming a scientist doesn't in reality fit his impression of "cool". But at the end, he bounces with just as much excitement to the idea of changing majors.

By Nautic Von Horn

HANES BOXERS

Brother-in-law

Chris, I need to ask you something, but you have to swear you won't tell my sister, okay? On our honor as brothers-in-law. Brother-in-law handshake. Okay.

Man, if you told your wife, she'd tell mine, and that can't happen.

I'm at my wits' end. See, I found something – something I can barely talk about. It was in my underwear drawer. And it's not mine. It's some other guy's, Chris! Some guy's underwear, in my underwear drawer! And it's driving me crazy thinking that some other guy – But, before I really freak out, I got to thinking maybe somehow our wives were at the laundromat together and maybe one of yours got mixed in, somehow, with what my wife brought home. Could have happened, right? Things like that do happen, right?

So, bro, weird question, but I gotta ask. Do you wear Hanes boxers size 32?

NOTES:

Desperation, to the point where grasping onto any possible hope seems like the only course.

Is his wife cheating on him? That fear is too devasting to speak out loud.

Asking a guy, even your brother in law, about their underwear is normally a creepy subject that guys would stay away from. But he must overcome the embarrassment of talking about underwear, and the much worse embarrassment of admitting his wife may be cheating, in order to explore the hope.

DEAL?

Boy

This is awkward, huh? We both like the same girl.
At first, I didn't want her. I was just being her
friend cuz she liked Tom and she asked me for
advice on how to get him. I gave her some ideas.
She brought him lunch from home, got candy
bars for him after school, helped him paint the
theater sets. It took at least a month for her to
realize Tom wasn't responding at all.

I know she asked for your advice, too. Did you
tell her Tom's gay? I mean, she liked him so
much, and I just couldn't say it.

Then, along the way, somehow, I started getting
into her. And you, too, huh? I could tell. Oh, man.
What are we going to do about it? She's not worth
blowing our friendship over, but ... well, I mean,
she's cute, and fun, and I really like her.

Alright, here's the deal. We each try our best until
Christmas break. Then whoever is in the lead, the
other steps out. Deal? Deal. May the best man
win.

I got Friday, already. No seriously, I already asked
her. You got her concert tickets, and she's going to
call me? Oh, no fair!

NOTES:

They say sometimes the chase is the best part.

This is classic high school. Maybe college age, too?

The two talking have been good friends for a long time. He means it when he says he doesn't want to ruin their friendship. But as the saying goes, "All's fair in love and war." When he says, "May the best man win" that is his declaration of war.

Too bad his friend has already won the first battle by getting concert tickets and convincing the girl to call off Friday's date!

THINK BIGGER

Student

I'm gonna be a huge star. The next Michael Jordan. I'll make millions. How much do you make, Mr. Von Horn? Teachers get like what, 30,000 a year, right? My boys in high school are already making twice that just standing on corners watching. They don't have to do no real gang stuff, just watch. And they're driving BMW's. I saw you driving your old cruddy VW Bug this morning. Man, you need new tires. What I wish? I wish they'd use us 8th graders cuz then I could do that and play basketball.

Science is cool and all, but where are you coming from, Mr. Von Horn, telling me to study? I got all my day busy training. I got hoops before school, at lunch, and after school. I'd play all night if my uncle let me stay out. And here's you wanting me to be a scientist? You went to college, right? You go to high school, you go to college, and here you are. Right here, in this dump. Chump change, Mr. Von Horn. You need to think bigger.

NOTES:

Yes, I taught 8ᵗʰ grade science in Watts, California, where I had many students exactly like this. I sure hope they went on to experience good and happy lives, but the odds were against them.

There truly were high school aged kids driving brand new Mercedes, BMW's, and other luxury cars around. As a teacher making thirty grand, it was very difficult to convince the students that they should study hard in 8ᵗʰ grade, so that they could move on to study hard in high school, so that they could study hard in college, and maybe someday do as well as I was!

We know, of course, the chances of becoming the next pro basketball star making millions are slim to none, while the chances of going to jail for gang-related crimes are much larger. But this student does not see it that way. That's not to say the student is blind or dumb – far from it. The kids in inner city environments like Watts know exactly what's up. Many of them had seen more in their young lives than I ever will. It's raw determination and spirit that drives them.

Also, hatred of the system. It's not their fault they were born into that type of world, and this student is pointing out how messed up it is that the teacher who studied and did all the "right stuff" in the system is the one with a low-paying job driving an old beater car.

ME AGAIN

Man

Hi! Yeah, it's me, again. I wasn't here for lunch yesterday because you were off, and there's plenty of other restaurants within walking distance of my office. But you know I'm going to come in every day that you are here. Just to give you a chance to answer that question I asked last week.

Is today the day? While you're thinking I'll have the BLT, with the regular iced tea. You know, if the answer is "no" just tell me. I can always eat somewhere else.

Something has been bothering me, and I have to get it off my chest because I wonder if it may be bothering you, too. I usually tip much better than what I've been giving you. I just didn't want you thinking a big tip was a bribe to go out with me or me showing off. Of course, if you were going out with me then I could tip better.

If I stay for dessert today do you think you'll make up your mind by then? I'm just asking because the place on the corner has a cherry pie special today. It's pie day over there. So, if you're going to say no, can you let me know in time to still get over there for the special?

NOTES:

Creepy? Or lovingly desperate?

Do you suppose he has prospects at the other restaurants?

You might play this one for comedy, or make it full out creepy, or perhaps go for pity. Poor guy, just wants to know if he should stick around and miss pie day.

By Nautic Von Horn

BETSY'S ANXIETY

Woman

My dog has a lot of anxiety attacks. You're good with that, aren't you? I can't leave her here if she's not going to get all the comfort and attention she needs.

I'm sure it's traumatic to be groomed. Think about it! Total strangers prodding and clipping and scrubbing all your intimate spots. Clipping hair all over your body. You sure you do a good job? I know you're licensed and the Better Business Bureau rates you highly and your Facebook page has a lot of likes and Herbert's Meat Market let you post your card on their bulletin board, which they don't do for everyone, and my sweet old neighbor recommended you - Mrs. Bertlemeister, with the standard poodle - but will my Betsy like you?

I'm sorry to ask so many questions but like I said my dog has anxiety problems. She can't relax. She's high strung, hyper, and really uneasy talking to strangers or going new places or trying new things. She's a bundle of nerves.

Alright then, if you say so. Listen, my phone will be off. I'm going to my spa, over in the Hills. I can wait to the end of the day to pick Betsy up, can't I?

NOTES:

Supposedly, dogs and their masters are much alike. This woman describes her dog as the one with anxiety attacks, but it seems she's describing herself.

Which sets up the ending. After all her concern about Betsy, she ends with wanting to be sure that she can relax all day at the spa without being bothered.

WE'VE HAD ENOUGH

Roommate

Ted, got a minute? I was talking with Mike at
lunch before you got up and we pretty much
decided. You can talk to him, too, but he just left
to work out. He wanted me to say this to you
when you got up.

Do you even remember last night? I think you
came in around four. I tried to get back to sleep
with my head under the pillow and at some point
I looked at the clock. Mike said you woke him up
around 4:30. Shit, I bet it took me an hour to get
back to sleep.

It's cool, man, that you're getting all these gigs,
and I know you think Mike and me are jealous
that your career's taking off, and not ours, but
that's not it. I don't care anymore that you
dumped us out of your band; you had your
reasons, although dude I'm shitloads better now
than I was then. I've been practicing like you'd
never believe. Look at these calluses!

But Ted, here's the thing. You been hitting it hard.
I can't tell if you're sober even now. The partying.
The late nights - do you have to make so much
noise coming home? Mike, Mike and I, we
decided this morning, we've had enough. He's
going to have his parents kick you off the lease.

First of next month. Hey, you hear me, Ted? I can help ask around for you to get a new place. We're friends, right? No hard feelings. But Mike's had enough. You got to move out.

Ted? Hey, Ted, are you listening? Ted?

NOTES:

Nope, pretty sure Ted's not listening. He's convinced his loser roommates are ganging up on him because of their jealousies, and he's probably already been thinking about moving.

Mike was too cowardly to say this directly to Ted, so it falls on you to deliver the bad news. And yet, you're torn between wanting Ted out so you can sleep and envying his lifestyle. You'd jump at a chance to get back into Ted's band! That's why you've been practicing so much lately.

In fact, you think Mike is the real loser. The only reason to stick with Mike is the fact that his parents own the house where you rent a room. Mike's off wasting time at the gym, while you were staying in to practice. You should be a star, and if Ted would only give you another chance ....

SAY THAT AGAIN

Teenager

Mom, say that again. I didn't hear right ....

Jesus, Mom! Ten years! Dad died ten years ago and you're just now telling me he left a suicide note! One you never read?!

How - what - how could you not read it? How could you not tell us kids, give us a chance to read it, let us hear in Dad's own words what he killed himself for. Jesus! My father's last words!

Were you afraid about what's in there? Are you afraid? Afraid he did it because of you?

Mom, get it. Get it out, now. Get it for me, let me read it. I have a right! He was my father. After all this time let me find out why, please. All these years not knowing, wondering if it was something I did, if it was my fault. I know it wasn't. It wasn't. My therapist told me, I didn't pull the trigger. But, Mom. Let me find out. Let me know.

Don't worry. If it's bad I won't tell you.

NOTES:

Nothing's more powerful than family dynamics. Kids vs. parents, parents vs. each other, living vs. dead memories.

Shock and disbelief rule here. The very idea that the father left a note never crossed this child's mind ten years ago, when the teenager was 5 years old, or so. Now, the shock to discover that there is a note truly rocks this teenager's world.

And the double shock that it was hidden all these years by the mother! Shock, betrayal, anger, righteous entitlement – something must be done immediately.

At the end is a bit of compassion. It won't be easy to read this note, no matter what your therapist told you, and you realize it won't be easy for your mother to hear it, either.

I WOKE UP THIS MORNING, DEAD

Man

I woke up this morning, dead.

You're right. I'm going crazy, and of course I know it's not healthy for me! I'm sorry. I don't mean to yell at you. I've been hiding in this apartment for three weeks since the funeral. Three weeks of hell. Three weeks in denial. I simply couldn't believe she's gone.

But then last night was the roughest yet. Two - three - bottles of wine and I could finally face it. In vino veritas! I passed out but when I woke up this morning, I clearly remembered my last thought: she's dead. She's dead. And that means I'm dead. Dead inside. Dead to the world. Every little bit of joy in this life went with her. Every reason I had for living is in a box in the ground!

You know, the damn phone's been ringing nonstop - texts, emails, crap! But you're the first at my door, coming in person to check on me.

Thank you!

NOTES:

Did you tear up, reading this? If not, read it again.

Every reason to live is buried in a box, out of reach forever. This man is not suicidal, but that leaves him in pure hell, stuck inside his apartment with literally zero reason for going on in life. If love is dead, then so is he. That's how strong his love was (is).

Yet, he knows life must somehow go on, someday. He's ignored countless phone calls from people trying to reach him. He's shut himself off from the world. But, deep inside, he is desperate to find new meaning in life.

The person at his door may be a good friend, and may even be someone who could become a new love interest. Either way, by coming to his door that person has thrown him a lifeline.

Confessing his pain, his denial, his turning to the bottle is his way of releasing the past and grabbing the proffered life line. "Thank you!" is so many things: choosing life, turning from death, expressing true appreciation (even love) that this person cared enough to come, crawling up from the darkness of despair to grab desperately at the light of hope.

By Nautic Von Horn

BACK ON

Cop

I'm turning off the recorders. See? Right now, there's no one on the other side of that glass. No one can see or hear us now. We can talk freely. You don't believe me. Naturally, you think this is some cop trick. I waltz in here, kick out the cops that have been interrogating you, and lie to you about the equipment to get you to incriminate yourself. Sure.

But there's something you don't realize, Tommy. I already know you're guilty. Yeah, I know you're a contract killer. These other cops don't know that. I don't need no confession. How do I know? Think about it.

I know for the simple reason that I hired you. 32,000 for the hit, provided it was done by Saturday. Sound familiar? No. No one knows I work here, and you ain't going to tell no one. You think I'm alone in this? Guess again. We're everywhere. Think about it. We can reach you here, in the depths of New York City's finest holding tank. You weren't supposed to get arrested, you moron. But listen. We can pull strings to get you out. Just clamp your damn mouth shut tight and keep it that way. Have patience.

You fuck with me and I got at least twelve guys who'll gladly shank you in jail before morning. And then, we'll go after your sister, too, and her kids. Think about it, Tommy.

Shhhhhhh. Back on.

NOTES:

Oh, boy. A villain! Yes, it's fun to be the evil villain.

Poor Tommy took a job and got caught. That's bad enough, but imagine his horror to be approached like this while in the custody of New York's finest. The message is clear: no place is safe from this criminal organization.

You ordered a hit. You yourself are not a contract killer. Not to say you're a saint, but you're too smart to be the frontline killer; you are the evil genius pulling strings from behind the scenes.

Knowing how to get into the police detention room, send the honest cops out, and turn off the equipment for a private chat is child's play for you. And that's what is so cold about the message for Tommy. He's got to believe you mean every word you say.

By Nautic Von Horn

SORRY ABOUT THE FEATHERS

Neighbor

Hey, Fred. Yeah, howdy neighbor. You know, this barb wire I put on top of the fence isn't stopping your cat from getting my birds. I've seen her over here three times today, and look, there's nary a goldfinch anywhere. I've got some crap jays and the regular mourning doves, but the little songbirds aren't coming to my feeders anymore. They're scared, I suppose, or worse.

Too bad you're not a dog person. This fence would be fine for dogs, but your cat still climbs it. You ever consider switching to a dog? Maybe a nice husky? I'm sure they'd take your cat down at the shelter, find it a good home.

I'll figure out something. I saw an automatic system that fires bb's -- hey, I'm kidding. Still, good fences make good neighbors, right? And I've already made this as high as code allows. I'm thinking electric. You wouldn't mind fried cat, would you? I'm kidding! Still, you have your yard the way you like it, and you like cats; I just think I ought to have my yard the way I like it, and I like birds.

Your yard is a bit messy today. Sorry about all the feathers.

NOTES:

Good fences are supposed to make good neighbors. But what if the effect of what the neighbor is doing (i.e., owning a cat) is not stopped by a fence?

You've tried so much. You're at your wits end. Maybe you have seriously thought about shooting the neighbor's cat. You've schemed about how to do it in a way that can't be traced to you. Maybe poison is the answer. But you love birds, and that's because you love all animals, all life. You couldn't actually hurt the cat.

Well, maybe you could hurt the cat just a little bit – just enough to scare it away from your yard. BB's or electric shocks. You're seriously thinking of it, although you don't dare tell the neighbor, and you're afraid of legal repercussions.

So, what to do?

Memorization tricks

If you can remember the lyrics to your favorite song, you can memorize any of these monologues. It just takes a little effort. Some people have success with these tricks.

<u>Emotions</u>. The essence of acting is understanding your character fully, so that you can *feel* the character's emotions. Write down every emotion you think your character is feeling. Decide which are the strongest emotions and memorize the order of those, then try to improv the piece just based on those emotions.

<u>Beats</u>. The "beats" are the parts of your monologue where something, usually emotion, changes. Like an outline. If you tear the work apart and analyze it, so that you understand the beats, you'll find it easier to remember what you're doing. For example, in the first monologue the Sheriff is reacting to having been called a "killer" by telling his origin story. Then he switches to justifying the need for his actions. The more you analyze and break down a scene to understand its subtext, the easier it is to remember.

<u>Bullet Points</u>. Closely related to the above, this method is like outlining an essay. Sum up each paragraph with two or three words. Then memorize that outline. I'm working on one now where the paragraphs can be summed up as "I'm here", "Fight!", "I'm sorry", and "I understand." It's easy to remember that much, and

with that guideline clear in my head I can begin to flesh it out further.

Singing. Something about putting words to music clicks into a different part of our brains. Hum along with the monologue. Pick a melody you know or make up a new tune. You won't perform it that way, but the words may come easier.

Writing. Similarly, if you write the words out long hand, you activate different parts of your brain. Just like taking notes in class helps you later recall what the teacher said. Write your monologue out carefully, to be sure you have it correct. Then write it again without looking at the source material. Keep doing this until you can write the whole thing out without errors.

Sleeping. Many people are at their most creative when just falling asleep, or just waking up. I have often run through monologues at night, as the last thing I do before falling asleep. (Actually, repeating them will help you fall asleep.) And then again, first thing I do in the morning, before getting out of bed. This is a great way to learn monologues, and also to keep them fresh in your head. When you know 9 or 10 monologues, you'll want to regularly run through them so that they remain fresh in your head.

Driving / Walking. At the risk of seeming odd to passersby, running through monologues as you travel around is a great use of your time.

"Stacking" is a memory technique where you learn the work in bitesize chunks. Maybe a sentence at a time, or a beat. Memorize the first before going on to the second. Then do the first with the second part until you have both down, and then add the next part. Keep stacking the parts until, presto, you got it all.

First Letters. Write down the first letter of each word on a piece of paper. You'll end up with a long string of letters. Then see if you can "read" it just looking at those first letters.

First Words. Write down the first two words of each sentence, then "read" the whole thing.

Repeat After a Break. Try memorizing, then take a break and come back an hour later to memorize again, and then again after another hour break. The gap in the process actually helps our brain rewire itself.

Videotape or record yourself. When you start the camera or sound recorder, try to do the whole thing even if you can't recall the correct words. Get the gist of it. Then watch the video with the script in front of you and see what you need to work on.

Friends can help you by listening. It does wonders to have an audience to focus your attention. They can also help by running the other character lines.

"There's an App for that." It's called Actor Trade, and it's free. The way it works is that you can help other actors learn their lines, and every minute you donate in that manner is a credit for you to ask other actors to help you. While your friends may be willing, friends are sometimes not very good in reading lines well – unless they themselves are actors. With the app, you can get excellent actors to read the other lines, and it helps greatly to have those lines read with meaning and emotion.

Subconscious. You know how people have great ideas in the shower? Or in bed? Or as they're driving? When we're busy doing something else, our minds can be more receptive to thinking on a different level. Whenever you're doing something that doesn't require your full attention, try running through your monologue.

And, finally, the method that works best:

Repetition. Repetition. And repetition. Nothing beats good old fashion repetition. Repetition.

Repetition. Repetition. And repetition. Nothing beats good old fashion repetition. Repetition.

Tips on getting auditions

We've talked about how to perform a winning audition monologue, but how do you get the auditions in the first place? Here are some tips:

<u>Don't sell yourself short</u>. Sometimes we see casting notices and think, "Nah, I could never do that." Or "That just isn't me." Or "they'd never take me." But instead, why not try it? Have fun and push yourself a bit out of your normal comfort box.

<u>Embrace open call auditions</u>. Sometimes called "cattle calls", open auditions are the type posted generally and for which you can expect hundreds or thousands of people submit. But don't let thoughts of numbers or odds deter you. Someone gets the role!

<u>Show up</u>. Success is 90% showing up (a quote sometimes attributed to Woody Allen). You won't find opportunities laying on the coach eating potato chips. Push yourself to get involved in local shows, events, festivals, club meetings, podcasts, student films, etc. Get out there, in real life.

<u>Piggyback</u>. When you have an audition, ask the people you're meeting with what else they're doing, or what they're working on next. It might be that the next show they're developing is a better fit for you. And look around. If you go into a studio for an audition, maybe what's going on next door is worth looking into. You're already dressed and looking dapper, why not introduce

yourself to other groups? Even if they are filming already, they might need another actor.

Keep in touch. Be a good friend. When you meet someone, follow up with an email, or better yet an actual hand-written note! "Networking" is only slimy when you aren't sincere about your intentions. Be honest, be friendly, be kind, be nice, be sympathetic, be understanding. Sure, you might not have been chosen for a certain project, but it can't hurt to keep in touch so they think of you on the next!

Create your own website. On your own site you (and only you) are in full control of how you are presented. Post your headshots. Announce your successes as you get each role. Be entertaining. And then post the link to your site on social media, or hand it out in real life.

Find ways to show your reel. You have a reel, right? If not, make one! An actor's reel is a short compilation of their best work, just 3-5 clips at the most and each no longer than 20 seconds. Simple editing; no need for fancy transitions or glitzy lighting / sound effects. Put your reel on YouTube or Vimeo and post the link to it on your website and social media. Send the link to people. Hand out cards with a QR code that goes to your reel. And keep your reel updated, with the work you are proudest of always in the first position.

Be a "Local". Watch for shows being filmed anywhere near you, and reach out (in person, by telephone, through social media, by contacting mutual friends, etc.) and let them know that you are a local. Productions on location travel with only the top actors and top crew positions. Since they have to pay for transportation, hotel and meal costs for those people, they will try to keep the size of the entourage down. That means they will want to hire locals as much as possible. Being local is a good thing for them, as you save them money! Every production on location hires at least one person to find people like you; make it easier for them to find you by posting your availability and working your connections to get to them.

Put yourself out there. Create content and post it on YouTube, Facebook, Instagram – anywhere and everywhere! You never know when someone will see something and want to see more. In today's age where basically every cell phone has a "broadcast quality" camera, and it cost nothing to post your work, you have no excuse not to.

Keep learning. Acting classes have double value for you. Classes keep your skills sharp AND you never know who you might bump into as part of the class or as part of the acting workshop presentations that are frequently put on by classes (and rumored to be attended now and then by casting directors).

Get referrals. In almost all other lines of business, having recommendations on your resume is important. But you rarely see that in the Entertainment World. Don't underestimate the value of referrals. Ask your class teachers if they know anyone they can refer you to. Don't be afraid to work connections and drop names.

Be the solution. Don't think of yourself. Instead, think about the problems that others are having, and find ways to help them. For example, casting directors have a huge problem: they must find good actors that fit certain roles, and they know the success of a project is often dependent upon the right casting. When you audition, don't focus on your own nerves and fears, but instead focus on their problem; present yourself to them as the solution they are looking for.

Play. Watch John Cleese's videos about the importance of play when it comes to fostering success. Play time opens up creativity and imagination. You might do better meeting people and auditioning if you remove the pressure you're feeling. Just relax and have fun. Play.

Be real. The Entertainment World already has plenty of fake people; why not try to be something different? Be your own authentic self. Don't kiss ass or only say what you think people want to hear. If you do "you" then you will find people that appreciate you and want to work with you.

Get on set. Almost every film and tv set needs more PA's (production assistants) and it's a job you can easily learn to do. Being part of a production can help you in countless ways: you learn things, meet great people, have fun, make some money … and also, if they need another actor, you're right there!

Go for background and extra work. Some actors think such work is beneath them, but it's the kind of exposure and opportunity to network that should not be passed up.

<u>Give back</u>. When you get a little success under your belt, remember others. Post encouraging words, give credit to others, remember that no one (not even you) succeeds in a vacuum.

<u>Media</u>. Be a guest speaker on podcasts – they are always hungry for guests! Send a note to tv and newspaper reporters – they are frequently looking for human interest stories.

<u>Get lucky</u>. Easier said than done, right? We all know there is an element of luck in all walks of life, and sometimes the difference between success and struggling to make it hinges on the most unlikely set of events. But embrace good luck. If something happens, follow up on it. Don't be shy about accepting luck when it comes your way.

<u>Be confident</u>. Have you heard people say that they make their own luck? Meaning that much of what we call "luck" is actually attitude. Be confident! Not egotistic. Confidence (the right kind) comes from training and practice. Rely on your training and practice; it's much better than luck! Let your confidence carry you through the rough patches.

<u>Be ready</u>. Opportunity knocks, but when the door opens you can only walk through if you have trained and practiced enough to be ready.

<u>Give the little guys a chance</u>. Many times, a seemingly "nothing" casting notice can lead to great experiences. A simple Facebook post, perhaps. Student films or indie

projects. Super low budget projects, even those that can't pay you anything. Everything you do will help you become a better actor, so why not?

<u>Keep cards handy</u>. Business cards, post cards, or whatever. You never know when you might bump into someone interested in your work.

<u>Meet people</u>. Meeting people, however you can, is a necessary part of marketing yourself. Take a job as a waiter or bartender where you will have plenty of chances to talk with people. Go to industry-related events, such as held by film groups and your local city Film Commission office. Volunteer at film festivals.

<u>Move</u>. Your hometown may not have many opportunities. Places like LA, New York City, and Atlanta have many productions going on every day. Sometimes you have to take a jump. BUT, please don't move until you are ready – in other words, train and practice BEFORE you move. Do virtual auditions and consider moving only after you are invited to the big city for one or more paying roles. Be smart about when to go, and how to live.

<u>Online casting sites</u> like Back Stage and Actors Access are worthwhile. They are becoming more and more legitimate. There was a time when the idea of paying an agency meant that it was a scam, but in today's world more and more talent agencies and online casting boards are operating on a paid subscription basis.

Break a leg

Get out there and make yourself into the successful actor you know you can be!

And please, let me know how this book has helped you. I'd love to hear your own stories about climbing the ladder to successes.

Post your monologues on YouTube or Vimeo, and send me a link. These monologues were written for YOU, so that you can perform WINNING AUDITIONS!

Break a leg, my friends.

~ Nautic

Nautic Von Horn

nauticproductions@yahoo.com

By Nautic Von Horn

www.ingramcontent.com/pod-product-compliance
Lightning Source LLC
Chambersburg PA
CBHW060325050426
42449CB00011B/2657